Laura

W9-AVO-748

August 1999

Purchased at a half price book
store in a Suburb of Dallas, TX.
for $5.

The
CREATION
of the
NIGHT SKY

Books by Nicholas Christopher

POETRY
The Creation of the Night Sky (1998)
5° (1995)
In the Year of the Comet (1992)
Desperate Characters: A Novella in Verse (1988)
A Short History of the Island of Butterflies (1986)
On Tour with Rita (1982)

FICTION
Veronica (1996)
The Soloist (1986)

NONFICTION
Somewhere in the Night: Film Noir & the American City
(1997)

ANTHOLOGIES (AS EDITOR)
Walk on the Wild Side: Urban American Poetry since 1975
(1994)
Under 35: The New Generation of American Poets (1989)

The
CREATION
of the
NIGHT SKY

POEMS

Nicholas Christopher

Harcourt Brace & Company

New York   San Diego   London

Requests for permission to make copies of any part
of the work should be mailed to: Permissions Department,
Harcourt Brace & Company, 6277 Sea Harbor Drive,
Orlando, Florida 32887-6777.

Library of Congress Cataloging-in-Publication Data
Christopher, Nicholas.
    The creation of the night sky: poems/by Nicholas
Christopher. — 1st ed.
        p.   cm.
     ISBN 0-15-100344-0
     I. Title.   II. Title: Xrays.
    PS3553.H754X17   1998
    811'.54 — DC21   97-36881

Text set in Electra
Designed by Lydia D'moch

Printed in the United States of America
First edition

E D C B A

Acknowledgments

Some of the poems in this book first appeared in the following publications:

The Paris Review: "In the Shadow of the Mountain," "Birds of Paradise in Ice Water," "On a Clear Night," "Della"

DoubleTake: "Jupiter Place, 1955"

The New Yorker: "Midsummer"

The Nation: "X Rays," "Antiquities"

Ontario Review: "Uncle Phillip's Funeral in Las Vegas"

Michigan Quarterly Review: "Rice Wine"

Graffiti Rag: "Suicide Watch," "Suburban Nocturne," "The Thirteenth Floor"

The Honolulu Advertiser: "Three Haiku: Haena Point, #1"

for Constance

Contents

The
CREATION
of the
NIGHT SKY

Part One

X Rays

A door creaks open
a few inches
and light the blue of the sea
streams in from far away
from beyond the sea

dividing this empty room
with its four sealed windows
one in each wall
and its floorboards
like bars of iron glowing

A woman with a skeleton on fire
a man in whose stomach
goldfish orbit a star
a boy who's swallowed buffalo nickels
a girl with an extra rib

come and go over the years
as well as those unfortunates
who enter supine
with cracked skulls or blotched lungs
their hearts fluttering to a standstill

while that familiar pair
the reticent man in black
the wispy woman in white
who brought you into this world
and will usher you out of it

work the machinery
in close conjunction and silence
from behind the door
their shadows flowing down the long corridor
out the window into the night

In the Shadow of the Mountain

at a broken table
ringed by potted flowers
between which the spiders have strung bridges
the women push back their chairs
leaving their cold soup untouched

The doors have been removed from their hinges
and the windows are boarded up
in anticipation of the hurricane
that will strip bare
the foliage along the green river

In the failing light dogs in packs
are roaming the beach
owls are streaming ashes from their wings
flowers heavy as stones
are sinking to the ocean floor

Whole slopes of this mountain will be torn away
the boulders where lizards bask at noon
and the banyan trees clotted with myna birds
and afterwards one of the women will return
to the broken table which has remained standing

among the flowerpots and chairs scattered
on the terrace newly laced with spiderwebs
and dip her broken fingers into the single
untouched bowl of soup feeling for the stone
the color of water she found on the mountain

many years ago and lost many years later
shaped like the mountain itself
whose inverted shadow darkening the valley
is approaching slowly now
like a hurricane

Midsummer

Bashō says the body is composed of one hundred bones and nine
     openings.
Within which flimsy structure the spirit dwells.

Floating by the park at dusk, through the heavy trees,
the white building glides like a ship.

An amber lamp is lit in a top-floor window
and a woman in her robe is leaning on the sill, eyes closed to the
     sunset.

A violet shadow is pouring down the side of the building from her
     long hair.
Two pigeons are perched in the next window, against a black room.

Beyond the trees, down a rough slope, the river is winding
around the island, flowing into the sea.

Slowly the mist off the river coils around the building, concealing it.
And just as slowly it lifts.

Only now the woman's lamp is extinguished.
Her window remains open, the curtain flutters,

but there is no sign of her, laid down to sleep in the darkness—
her pale body with its one hundred bones and nine openings

from which the spirit will one day slip, like the mist seeping
back through the trees, along the river, out to sea.

7

Antiquities

The hands of Franz Liszt were painted
in pale green on the battered armoire
in a storefront before which sand was sprinkled
and a pyramidal sign read ANTIQUITIES.
Objects many centuries older than antiques.

Yet nothing in that store dated back
to ancient Greece or Rome, to Egypt,
Assyria, or the Ch'in dynasty.
The oldest item was a set of cutlery
in a walnut case stamped 1899.

It was February and sleet was falling
on a sharp diagonal onto Second Avenue.
The wind skidded a black hat through the traffic.
A bell tinkled when I entered the store,
and removing my gloves, examined the armoire.

There was no one behind the counter,
just a beaded curtain leading into darkness
from which suddenly the stormy concluding
chords of Liszt's second Hungarian
Rhapsody echoed, as if they had traveled

through a succession of rooms,
down untold, twisting corridors—
like the labyrinth in the bowels of a pyramid.
To play those chords properly, a pianist
must possess Liszt's two-octave reach,

accurately rendered in the green hands
poised over their keyboard,
which I reached out to touch as the wind
blew open the door and rushed in,
extending that long final chord indefinitely.

Jupiter Place, 1955

The three sisters who lived in the house surrounded
by hedges elaborately set a redwood table in their backyard:
twelve miniature cups and saucers, plates, spoons, and forks,
on a white paper tablecloth the wind, at any moment,
threatened to lift skyward, where it would crumple,
then billow, indistinguishable from the clouds.
I had often wondered what went on behind those hedges
down the street: I knew the girls were twice my age—
I was four—and that I was the youngest
of the nine guests invited to their tea party;
the only other boy, around six, was someone
I had never seen before on our street.
He had hair pomaded so flat it shone like a mirror,
and on his starched collar he wore a clip-on bow tie.
"He's our cousin from Syracuse," the eldest sister informed me,
and, seated beside me, he didn't speak to anyone.
I had never heard of Syracuse, and even now I do not know
if he had journeyed from upstate New York or the coast of Sicily.
Expecting cake, I was served crab apples, acorns, and a pinecone,
and from the teapot an imaginary arc of "Darjeeling"—
the word rolled off the second sister's tongue—
filled my cup to the brim before she offered me
first a sugar bowl without sugar, then a pitcher and a yellow dish,
murmuring, "Cream or lemon," at which point, vastly
disappointed but getting the hang of things, I took an imaginary
wedge of lemon, squeezed it into my cup, and refrained
from biting into the one edible prop, my crab apple.
Then I noticed that the youngest sister had wandered

across the lawn and was dancing under an enormous
weeping willow, up high on her toes—
the first piece of ballet I ever witnessed—
trailing a chiffon shawl and tossing her dark hair
first over one shoulder, then the other.
The cousin from Syracuse looked away with set jaw,
and the other girls never left off their chattering,
but, empty cup raised to my lips, I couldn't take my eyes off her.
Every day after that, from my window or front walk,
I watched her amble past my house on the way to school,
loitering well behind the other children.
She must have always been late:
the bookbag in one hand and the lunch pail in the other
appeared to weigh her down terribly as she zigzagged
down the street from sidewalk to sidewalk,
pausing whenever a bird or flower caught her eye.
Never once did she speak to me, or I to her.
And I was not invited back for another tea party,
even though—unlike her cousin, who had nodded off unhappily—
I thought I had played my part well,
repeatedly emptying my empty cup with gusto.
Then, in the spring, I stopped seeing her altogether,
no matter when I planted myself at the window.
I worked up the nerve to ask her sisters about her,
but without replying they brushed past me.
Other inquiries I made came to nothing.
Until just before my family moved away that summer
when suddenly everyone on Jupiter Place was talking
about her in lowered voices, with veiled expressions,
for in those days there was still a stigma attached

to anyone who contracted polio—another word
I had never heard before but would forever associate
with the name of that girl who had danced slowly
into the twilight beneath the enormous darkening tree
even as her sisters cleared the table
and the rest of us were sent home.
A name I heard in a whisper twenty years later,
at the reenactment of an ancient festival on Rhodes,
when in the whirl of dancers moonlit in sheer robes
one collapsed by a precipice high over the sea;
a name I wanted to call out twenty years after that—
just today—as a woman on crutches passed me,
tossing her hair over her shoulder before disappearing
down the sidewalk, descending along the shadows
of the trees that ran like a ladder as far as I could see.
Kathryn.

Birds of Paradise in Ice Water

In this room where no one speaks above a whisper,
despite the absence of a sick or dying person
or the presence of anyone engaged
in a difficult or private task, a dozen
of the great flowers on their formidable stems
have been arranged in a glass pitcher before a picture
window looking down the long snow-covered street.

I have seen them growing wild by the hundreds
along a riverbank on a Pacific island.
As I dipped my oars silently so as not to frighten
birds from their perches, the flowers loomed suddenly,
the slashed-orange petals with their rainbow streaks
indeed like wings poised to take flight
through the curtain of mist descending the mountains.

The canopy on the glass building down the street
has frozen in place as the wind left it, curling upward,
like a wave cresting to break in the open sea,
and at the base of the vase what appeared to be clear stones
anchoring the stems are in fact ice cubes to keep the flowers crisp
as the day they were cut from steaming soil, under a fiery sky
in which hundreds of birds—brighter than fire—were wheeling.

Uncle Phillip's Funeral in Las Vegas

1.

No one came.
Bands of heat, like a rainbow, shimmered over the desert.
Two birds punctured a cactus with their beaks, drinking deeply.
A cloud the size of a silver dollar dissolved in the sun.
A woman in white, swinging her hips,
came out of the crematorium to meet the hearse.
She wore cherry lipstick and green mascara.
Her many bracelets clattered.
She introduced herself as the funeral director
and, smiling, swatted away a fly.

2.

He was a short, blustery man with blue eyes,
a barrel chest, and wavy white hair.
In his last days, putting away a fifth of Scotch daily
in a furnished studio overlooking a parking lot
in the Duke of Devon apartments,
he constructed a schooner inside a bottle,
which he left unfinished and labeled
"The Shipwreck in the Bottle."
This may have been his most inspired moment.

3.

At eighty-five, he smoked a corona every morning,
scanned the racing forms,
and watched the fights on television
with the sound turned off.

A man who in his youth had worked
as a stevedore and a bouncer,
who boxed for his supper in the makeshift rings
behind the stockyards on Lake Michigan,
he died in his sleep with a table fan ruffling the sheets.
Among his personal effects were a purple heart
awarded for valor in the Argonne forest in 1917,
an honorary badge from the Chicago Police Department,
a photograph of himself with Gene Tunney and Mayor Daley,
and the birth certificate of a daughter
(dated December 24, 1932, in Miami)
who died within a week, unnamed.

4.

None of his four wives survived him,
though the last was twenty years his junior,
and he had no other children.
In my childhood he sent me a hundred dollar bill
every Christmas, and once, on my birthday,
a pair of spats and an ebony walking stick.
Another year, there was a basket of mangoes
from San Juan and a telescope
with MONTE CARLO printed on the barrel.
When I was nine, summering at a house
in the mountains, he came to a family reunion,
arriving all the way from Detroit
in a chauffeur-driven Daimler with a box of kippers
(which he ate daily, for longevity),
a case of Johnnie Walker Black,
and a set of pool cues, though there was no pool table.

Also, one of his wives, a former showgirl
who sat on the front porch in a white dress
shooing away flies with a Japanese fan.

5.
His will, otherwise unremarkable, specified
that he be cremated at noon the day
after his death and that a recording of the Overture
to *Don Giovanni* be played in the chapel.
As the brief plume of smoke sailed into the sky
from the stack discreetly concealed by palms,
the funeral director sat alone in the rear,
oblivious to the music, and flipping open
her compact, inclining her head into the shadows,
applied lipstick to her parted lips.

The Anonymous Letter

suggests it was in a previous life
I emerged from a long tunnel
echoing sharply with horses' hooves

and a cradle moon just a sliver
in a bracelet of stars
was poised above the steep cliff

from which a cloud of birds veered
pitch-black toward the breakers
a ship's light rising and falling over the horizon

and someone on a bluff calling to me
the wind drowning out the words
I hear now years later when I approach the sea

Five Nights in February

1.

High over Times Square, above a column
of flashing advertisements, a black and white sign
that does not flash reads PLUTO.
God of money and of death
who oversees these streets, these towers,
this starless sky in which, astrologers predict,
his planet, in retrograde as the full moon wanes,
will wreak havoc with the fates of all wind-bent
snow-swept pedestrians who happen to be born, like me,
in the last week of this month, under the sign of the Fishes.
                                                    —*New York City*

2.

A frayed ribbon flutters over the heating vent
and the wind itself, like a frozen sheet of gauze,
is stuck fast to the window.
In this hotel room where nothing grows
the dust is green as pollen,
the fog seeping under the door smells of the sea
and the telephone after midnight rings every hour
on the hour, though when I pick it up the line is dead;
and just as punctually at those instants, down the corridor,
the ice cubes rumble in the heart of the ice machine.
                                                    —*Baltimore*

3.

I'm dining alone in an empty Japanese restaurant.
Before me, in a bowl of plum vinegar,
slices of octopus thin as paper float beside flower petals,
and flying fish eggs glitter on a lacquered board.
An ice storm has emptied the street as well.
In a shopping cart beneath a plastic sheet, a woman
has positioned herself as we were taught to do at school
in the fallout shelter: arms crossed, head tucked between her knees.
In my room, I pour whiskey over ice, and from the shadows
beyond the glow of the aquarium, watch a lone fish orbit slowly.

—*Washington, D.C.*

4.

Benedict de Spinoza was a lens grinder by trade.
Over the years, the glass dust aggravated his tuberculosis.
In *The Ethics* he proposed that *the human mind
cannot be absolutely destroyed with the body,
but there remains of it something which is eternal.*
From this, the darkest and least expansive hotel room yet,
I overlook a cemetery that predates the American Revolution.
Its occupants felt the same sun and breathed the same air as Spinoza.
Their headstones topple like rows of broken teeth whose whiteness—
starker than the snow's—is animated now and then by a shaft of
        moonlight.

—*Boston*

5.

Ice sprays out from the wheels of the speeding train.
Through a curtain of snow a few particulars catch the eye:

a bus chassis on the roof of a gutted factory;
a freshly splintered tree; a pyramid of fire on a frozen lake.
We streak past Staten Island, into a tunnel that is a night within the night.
There is also a Staten Island in the archipelago of Tierra del Fuego,
where icy mountain caps blaze at sunrise and sunset.
Tonight even the summits of Times Square are darkened—
except Pluto's sign, which is still flashing on my closed eyelids
when, hours later, downtown, I turn—restlessly—in my own bed.

—New York City

A Visitor

Who are you and what do you want here?
Upon your arrival, birds swooped into the trees,
dogs cowered in the bushes,
and the one cat stepped through her own shadow
on a wall and disappeared.

Because you could only have come from one direction—
across the lake that is not yet frozen—
some concealed their fear of you better than others.
Many took flight, strewing the road with their possessions.
Others emerged to offer you gifts, in vain,

while praying you would not carry them away
across the lake and the forest
to the icy mountains by the sea
where you began the long journey that has left
your eyes, hands, and stomach empty.

Now, instead of hair, black water is flowing
from your head, threatening to flood the fields,
to drown even the swiftest among us.
And still we'll have nothing to give you.
Not even a name.

The Car Parked on the Beach Road at Anini

1.

It is a 1953 Buick, solitary on the narrow shoulder,
with a license plate, dated the same year
and never updated, that reads HANNAH.
For days, for miles, no other cars pass.

2.

The windshield is tinted the dark
blue of the sea that frames it,
as if the rising tide has flowed out
to the road by night and filled up the car.

3.

Painted forest green, faded to lime,
its surface is powdered with dust and salt
from whose depths symbols flower:
a cross, a wheel, a blank eye beneath a tilted oar.

4.

The stars fleck the pocked chrome
of its bumpers and by moonlight the shadow
of a palm tree slides across the sand onto its hood:
a tattoo of wind-whipped fronds.

5.

In one of its hubcaps, bright circle within
the circle of a whitewall, a dog is reflected
pausing to sniff, raising his leg, reconsidering,
moving on as the tall weeds flutter.

6.
A spider's web sparkles on the radio antenna.
Dead mosquitoes speckle the grille.
A moth's wing adheres to one headlight.
All of these will be washed away by the squall on the horizon.

7.
In the pink and gray of dawn a woman combs
her wet hair in the outside mirror and shivers
as fog rolls off the sea, blanketing the road
moments before a car passes at high speed.

Suicide Watch

In a sea of shadows
a building of locked windows
in which each light burns with the same low intensity
a man in a room without doors
is watching television and being watched
on a monitor in the next room

Beside him flowers cut from paper are wilting
bleached the same pale blue
as his paper slippers and the thinly
striped robe he is wearing over thin
pajamas while sitting on a hard chair
his pockets stuffed with packs of gum

On the dark window images are reflected
off the television screen
two cars careering down a mountain road
a woman on a railway platform swooning
into the backdraft of a passing express
a mouse in a cartoon snatching cheese from a mousetrap

And then the screen goes blank and reflects only
the man rigidly poised with the lamps dimming
and all the light in the room flowing
into him so that he shines
stretching his arms out with upturned wrists
in a sea of shadows

Rice Wine

From a long bottle with a curved neck
she poured it on her feet when we began
our journey on the white road to the sea,

past the broken statues of horses lining the fields,
their eye sockets brimming with starlight
that slid like tears down their cheeks.

No one had told us how far we had to travel.
Or warned us about the hazards of that country:
crows with human voices that continued

our conversation when we lapsed into silence;
trees without roots that followed in our wake;
stones warm as blood that pulsed in our hands;

fire-colored vines that hissed to life
when the rain fell, and mountains so steep
the boulders tumbled down their faces night and day.

And then there were the muddy rivers
that snaked back on themselves,
so in a single week we might ford the same one

a dozen times, always finding the current faster
and the bank more slippery, until finally we arrived
at our destination, overhanging the sea on crumbling terraces:

———

a city busy with people and animals we never saw;
with a single granite building that had reproduced
itself millions of times along an enormous grid;

with parks whose concentric paths never connected,
and streets of powdered stone that flickered like canals;
a city in which we had anticipated slaking our thirst

only to be told the wells were dry;
from which we had hoped to embark by ship
until we found it possessed no harbor;

a city filled with vacant hotels where only by bribing
a string of clerks could we secure a room,
without a bed, or even glass in the windows,

where, at nightfall, while moonlight rushed
from the gutters, we heard those crows
complete the conversation we had long ago abandoned.

Then she poured us each a tumbler of rice wine
from that same bottle we had carried
with us all those months but never touched,

and in the darkness across the sea
like a match head a distant point flared to life:
a place we would never reach now,

where our names were being recorded
in a burning ledger and our images etched—
with terrible precision—in sand ground from mirrors.

On a Clear Night

In the Kyi Valley of Tibet, a snow-white desert
where an orchestra of lamas performs by starlight for the gods,
it is said that when we near death, and may least suspect it,
sorcerers disguised as people in our daily lives—
neighbors, postmen, shopkeepers—
steal a single breath from us, slip it into a bag,
and at the moment we expire deposit it
high in the mountains that hold up the sky.

Sometimes the sorcerers can assume the form
of someone even closer to us, a friend or relative,
or a lover opening her handbag on a street corner.
As you are doing now—while the strains
of an orchestra waft from a car radio—
rummaging for your comb, running it through your hair,
and then snapping the bag shut with a smile.
Taking my breath away.

Four Renga

1.

The palms are flapping on the beach,
fronds singed by the salt
the trade wind has carried
across the ocean three thousand miles
from the frozen north.

—June 3

2.

A man tosses a stone into the surf
and a pair of black dogs, alternating, fetch it.
I'm lying flat and still as down the beach
a cloud blows seaward and light
along the golden sand slides toward me.

—June 9

3.

The wind sweeps the terrace
spraying the window screen.
The curtain lifts fast and drops slowly.
Under the stars I drink a pitcher of ice water
and urinate hard beneath the 'ohi'a tree, which yesterday
        blossomed.

—June 9

4.

In this room a silent switch turns on a lamp
beside a bed miles away, illuminating an inkwell
green as the sea where someone who can't sleep casts
a wavering shadow by moonlight and calls out across the waves.
And no one answers.

—June 10

—Kaua'i, 1995

Election Day

As the polls open, the skywriters
are drinking black coffee from tin
cups clinked so many times
in silent toasts that they are covered
with nicks, indiscernible except
in the darkness, where they glint like stars.

In their single-engine planes the skywriters
taxi down a dusty runway and spiral
up over the sprawling metropolis,
falling into a V-formation
before releasing the hyphens
of vapor that one by one form

letters, words, and finally an emphatic
message to millions of voters
which begins dissolving minutes later
beside the crescent moon,
a shell of itself in the morning light,
leaving nothing but shimmering sky.

Suburban Nocturne

Down a street where a single lamp is burning
in a window shrunken by thick vines
all the other houses are one with the darkness

like the pin oaks blotted against the starless sky
the dogs crouched under bushes who do not bark
at intruders and the cats on the ridges of sloping

roofs who remain invisible creeping
along the gables while the owls huddling
camouflaged scan the hard lawns for mice

From that lit window the same snatch of a cello
solo endlessly repeating on a scratched record
hisses through the vines into the wind

that is always from another place
cold when the street is hot and hot when it is cold
flowing through slowly every night

over the parallel lines of parked cars white
with dust from roads that no longer exist
and when that fragment of light and music is also gone

when shadows liquefy into shadows the darkness
complete finally after so many years
who will emerge from these empty houses to populate it

The Burn

After the woman we were visiting in Miami Beach
when I was six drank Eclipse rum far into the night
and waking with the shakes the next morning
spilled scalding coffee on my arm as I was gazing
out the window at the palms and buttering my toast,
after the emergency room doctors treated me
with ice and antibiotics while the woman sobbed
in the waiting room, sneaking sips from a flask
and smoking Lucky Strikes in a jade holder
yellowed with nicotine down the center,
my grandmother took me in a taxi on a road
lined with palms, tall and black for miles, to a man
in a solitary house at the edge of a swamp
who she said could heal burns so they left no scars—
which was more than the doctors could promise her.
It was nightfall, but still so hot that steam
was rising off the puddles by the road
and catching in the mangrove bushes, like cotton.
The house was dark, more shadow than light flowing
from the lamps, and filled with stuffed birds—
herons, owls, kingfishers—whose glass eyes
and curled leathery feet I examined closely.
The man had two broken teeth in front.
His hair was parted in the middle, combed flat.
His shirt cuffs were greasy and his cardigan nearly buttonless.
His lips were fixed in a thin smile, but his creased,
heavy-lidded eyes never once smiled.
My grandmother fanned herself on a threadbare sofa

in her flowered dress and white sandals and drank tea,
stirring in a spoonful of hibiscus honey,
while he sat me down at a cluttered table
in front of a fireplace stacked full of books:
with a mortar and pestle he ground up seeds and twigs,
mixed the powder into a bowl of brown liquid,
and with a spatula applied the salve to my burned arm.
He waited several minutes, smiling and gazing sadly
into my eyes, then coated the salve with a red jelly
that smelled so foul I gagged before he wrapped gauze
around my arm, taped it, and gave me
a bitter green lozenge to slip under my tongue.
I was to take a lozenge every six hours for six days,
at which time my grandmother was to remove
the bandage and rinse off the salve with cool milk.
These directions he scratched on a card in a cramped script,
identifying the lozenges as "essence of palm oil."
My grandmother handed him some money,
which he refused, and told me to say thank you,
and he never said a word, seeing us to the door,
past the shelves of dusty staring birds,
the bottles of smoke and herbs, the jars and urns,
and the guttered candles abandoned everywhere.
The taxi was still idling in front, blanketed with mist
through which he shone a flashlight down the path
tangled with roots and thorns, and he finally stopped
smiling as he nodded good-bye and we drove away
and his house was swallowed up by the night.
I asked my grandmother if he was a mute.
"Not exactly," she replied, as we sped back between

those rows of black palms under a swirling sky.
She explained that during the war, on a Pacific island,
he was trapped in a burning forest
from which he was the only soldier to escape.
"After that, he stopped speaking."
Back at her apartment, the woman who had spilled
the coffee was still drinking rum and smoking on the small
terrace where you could hear the ocean but couldn't see it.
My grandmother packed our bags and we moved to a hotel,
and only years later did I learn that the woman
had been that man's wife and that my grandmother
had known them before the war when they lived
on a peninsula, in a house encircled by palms,
where the wind never stopped blowing.

Six days after we visited him,
my grandmother unwrapped the gauze and washed off
the salve with cool milk and in the bright fluorescence
of the bathroom there was no sign of the burn.
No scarring.
Just a tiny mark—to this day it reappears on occasion—
which under a magnifying glass was revealed
to be the silhouette of a palm
on fire.

On Naxos

A beautiful girl wearing a T-shirt that reads ARIADNE
CAFÉ flies by on a motor scooter, her black hair streaming,
head tilted back just so drinking in the wind as she circles
the statue of Dionysus entwined with vines that casts a wine-colored
shadow in the cool square bearing his name where the vintners
are closed for siesta and the lobby of the Labyrinth Hotel—
its windows shuttered day and night—echoes with flutes and timbrels,
bells and the cries of dancers spinning through the darkness
in a long unbroken line down broken corridors to a room
where hooves are clattering on tiles and a moon
of hammered silver each night waxes and wanes on the cold wall.

Victim of Circumstances

Who can say that he, like all the rest of us,
will not fall into the machinery
of someone else's plotting, gone awry.
Leaving behind his own plots to entangle the lives
of others years after his destruction.
Will anything else survive him—
the contents of his mind, or of this room,
or the details of his worldly transactions—
any longer than the cigarette ash he flicked
last night that remains suspended in a spider's web?

Through his window he looks over the river
that snakes swirling like smoke
past the twinkling factories to the leaden sea.
From the street he hears a broken trumpet solo,
the echo of a girl singing before the bakery's oven,
rain spattering the parked cars.
Green tea steeps on his table beside a box of Spanish coins.
There is also a cigarette lighter without a wick, an astrolabe,
and the guts of an old radio with one tube blinking.

With these elements countless scenarios might be drawn
by an experienced housemaid or a rookie detective.
With the elements on the periodic table tacked to the wall,
sun-faded, water-stained, everything is possible:
from hydrogen that fuels stars to neptunium dense as stellar ash,
from nitrogen that infuses all living tissue to plutonium—
the stuff of Pluto—a pint of which could desolate the Pacific Ocean,

and thallium, with its vernal name (from the Greek
for "green shoot") so toxic it can fell a man in seconds.

One day the man will be sitting at the table by the window
when a woman screams at another window
and the wind carries her scream over the rooftops
to the river and then a door slams and someone runs
down the corridor and drops something heavy outside
his door which after several seconds, the breath caught
fast in his throat, the man stands up to open, realizing
this is the moment that has awaited him for years
and in the eternity it takes him to cross the room
knowing that afterward his life will never be the same.

Sleep

for Constance

In this blue room, behind salt-streaked shutters, you sleep,
the corner of the pillowcase beside your lips fluttering.
A spider is suspended from the ceiling fan,
and on the beach storm winds are lashing the breakers.

Today a cluster of black birds alighted, squawking, in a tree
dotted with red flowers beneath which I was sleeping.

Close by, the waves were sliding in through sheets of light,
and in the clouds a blue room appeared, identical to this room
in which I wind my way to sleep each night watching that spider spin.

Over the coast of this island, far from any continent, Antares,
the red star at the heart of Scorpio, is glowing brightly.

At dawn you will tell me how you saw that star from out at sea,
like a drop of blood in the night sky, as you tried to steady
your tossing skiff and return to shore, where loud birds
filled a solitary tree beside which I stood, waving you in.

Della

After washing your face and leaving it
in the basin of water from which it stared
up at you as you left the room,

you went out into the world where perfect
strangers coming up dazed from the river
waved to you through the deep sunlight.

This was the day on which you passed
the boy with the bandaged hands who wore
a placard that read EYES EXAMINED—50¢,

and the grim young woman in heels and shorts
pushing the empty stroller around
the parking lot in diminishing circles,

and the man in the cardboard box striding into
traffic swinging a plastic lantern, like Diogenes,
and the blind vendor in the skullcap roasting

almonds in honey by the hotel where the married
couple (each married to someone else) who had become
the morning headlines were found back to back under

icy sheets after sharing a bottle of sleeping pills,
and the breezy clerk with ink-stained fingers
and zip-up boots playing ticktacktoe on the #2

———

express train beside the pregnant girl
who was dreaming openly with an upturned face
and parted lips, hands clasped on her belly;

this was the day your friend Della disappeared
and no one—not friends, family
(her half-sister who hired a shady detective),

or finally the police—ever found her.
And for years, while waiting for the postcard
or phone call from some other city that never came,

you will pick over the details of all you saw
after setting out to meet Della that morning,
arriving at her apartment to find the door open

and her few possessions undisturbed,
her caged bird singing by the window and the sink
full of clear water in which you glimpsed

your face again, just as you had left it
in the room across town, but changed, even then,
before you knew you would never see Della again.

Three Haiku: Haena Point

1.
A strip of bark peeled
away like skin, and the pulp
of the hau tree dry.

—July 1993

2.
A bird clear as glass
skimming blue waves swoops upward
lost against the sky

—June 1994

3.
Under a cloud-blocked
sun the cool wind lifts me now
beneath spinning leaves

—May 1995

Divorce

In the solitary house in an open field
hidden objects have been brought out
and placed on the floor of the bedroom:

half a pair of scissors;
a thimble filled with worn phonograph needles;
a triangular stamp from a country that no longer exists.

All the windows are open.
On the taut bedcovers a woman is lying on her back
counting the birds in flight painted on the ceiling.

In the corner a man in a rocking chair grips his knees.
A storm is approaching and the sky has darkened
to the same purple as the woman's irises.

No points anywhere can be connected, she remembers
saying, as the rain, sharper than needles, slants
through the windows, filling the air with broken lines.

Where She Drowned

On the path of broken shells through the forest,
light pours from the door of a shack

where someone spooned tea leaves into a black pot
and left a kettle whistling on the stove.

The clock on the shelf has not been wound for years,
but just now it began ticking.

Down the beach, where the wind sharpens
itself along the sickle curve of the bay,

where the clouds have parted jaggedly
on some stars streaking earthward,

where the sheets of foam hiss
over stones glowing like embers,

the sea swallows a woman in a rush of steam,
her hair marbled like a wave about to break.

Night Train

Riding on silent rails through the desert,
when the cool winds blew down from the mountains
I tasted seawater in the back of my throat.
Billowing clouds obscured the moon
while the other passengers dissolved into mist
and the conductor into a wisp of vapor
at the head of the aisle
that like a river of darkness began to flow.

Closing my eyes, I was approaching the island
to which I have often returned,
but this time on a vast ship whose deck streamed
directly from the sun low across the water;
it would have taken me many days
to walk its entire length.
Sand poured from the sky, stinging like rain,
and in seconds filled the sea,
so that even the deepest currents, where the stingrays glide,
turned to glass and splintered into light,

lighting up in my head for an instant
as the train thundered onto a bridge
and crossed a ravine the fact
that a man's life
is an arc which twice intersects the horizon,
at birth and death—
at the one end a sea, at the other a desert,
both, from a distance (which is all the rest of his days),
shimmering, indistinguishable, seemingly endless.

The Thirteenth Floor

She said she had learned in another city
how to unblock the *manipura chakra*
(where the blood quickens just below the heart)
presided over by the whirling deities Vishnu and Lakshi

We were in a downtown building among swirling
black clouds at the center of the valley
where the sizzling grass grew chest-high
beneath the stars in the centuries before

first a village and then this city were erected
a building in which the elevators ran directly
from the twelfth floor to the fourteenth
but we had slipped off on a floor in between

At that hour there was no one on the treeless boulevards
or in the bare quadrangles that once were parks
(soil had become so scarce it could only
be found in basements with buckled floors)

In the locked room she turned down the lamp
while my eyes slid from the tinted windows
the skyline twinkling without lights
to her eyes in which a vast plain was burning

Lost and Found

For every object here a thousand others
are lodged in obscurity, by accident or design, never to be found:
the button off a vest slotted between floorboards,
the rusted penknife behind the warehouse sink,
the charm bracelet under the loose brick in the ivy-covered wall.
And still others vanish only to be recovered by someone else—
the hat that blows out the train window, spiraling crazily,
or the fountain pen dropped in a taxi which a subsequent passenger,
retrieving some coins, discovers behind the seat—
for whom they remain "found" objects,
often treasured for this reason
or else not especially missed if they're lost again.
Here where each thing has been found (but not kept)
it is considered lost until it is found again
by the person to whom it was last attached,
who must retrace his steps until he arrives at this warren
of shelves and aisles in a single spacious room
where the clerk posts his hours carefully
on the shuttered window, but rarely follows them,
opening late, closing early, or leaving for lunch and never returning.
Countless times he has lost the skeleton key that unlocks
the narrow door (the key always turns up again)
and each time picks the lock easily with a paper clip—
for it is a fact that, despite the many precious objects
it contains, the Lost and Found is never robbed.
As if possessions without a possessor—by some obscure
economic law—intrinsically lose their value.
And valuable or not, the longer they go unclaimed
the less coveted they become, until finally, when their official

46

lease (two years) on a bit of shelf space runs out
they may disappear once and for all with the trash.
But it's apparent that this seldom happens:
objects perched on the highest shelves have collected
decades' worth of snowy dust, camouflaging their true shapes
and functions—like the elements of a landscape after a blizzard.
The conical object in the corner might as easily be a wizard's
hat (imprinted with celestial bodies) as a small megaphone,
and the upturned disc on a pedestal could be a sundial or a
　　　　table fan.
For one of these, or a recent addition to the shelves,
a claimant must offer up some identifying features
or—better yet—defects that make it unique:
the trenchcoat with a tartan lining torn at the armpit,
the sterling cigar case with a zigzag scratch,
the monogrammed watch missing its second hand.
This description must be printed on an index card
in the presence of the clerk, who then attempts to match it
to one of the numbered cards in his file box.
In the Lost and Found each object has a number,
an age and place of origin, and a set of distinguishing marks,
just like the passport issued to a man or woman;
in fact, these objects are shown more dignity
than they may have known in their previous lives
as anonymous parts of some larger clutter—and certainly more
than that button, penknife, and bracelet (whose talismans
brought *it* no luck) relegated to oblivion in the outside world.
Granted longevity, spared wear and tear, they remain
in this limbo where they can never be lost again
so long as they are never found.

The Lights of Siena as Seen from Florence in a Dream

This is the door by which you will leave me forever.
As always, it stands ajar, admitting the cold
rays of stars that will help you navigate the darkness.

In an ink blot a woman in blue deciphered the future.
Not hers, or yours, but mine.
She wore earrings carved of bloodred stone:

hardened embers, highly polished, that sprayed
seaward from a volcano on the Tropic of Cancer
ten thousand years before her birth.

She offered me a glass of clear tea
and drew the curtains from a rain-streaked
window overlooking a broad expanse

in which the sun, minutes from setting,
was streaming flames over the horizon,
igniting the poplars like torches.

I walked all night along a road soft with dust.
The pack on my back was heavy as stone.
Faceless coins jangled in my pocket

and the hands on my watch were moving in opposite directions.
Like fingers, the wind ran through my hair.
Walking in step to my heartbeat, I crossed a vast plain

and took this hotel room in Florence where I saw
the lights of Siena far to the south, like the stars
that even then were leading you away from me.

A Line of Palms

leading to a circle of palms
through which the sunlight slants green with dust
and the yellow birds in a spiral
climb the notes of a flute
played by a blind man
beside a pyramid of boulders.

In the other direction, the palms run
straight to the sea, casting long shadows,
each of which ends in a circle of light
where a girl is balancing
a basket of shells on her head.

This is a circular city—like Alexandria,
like Nineveh when Sin, the moon god,
journeyed through the night sky
in a circular boat—where the zigzag
streets never intersect and the sea,
drained of color, defines no horizon.

In the park, monkeys and gazelles roam freely.
Roving violinists tune up, but don't play.
And the war cripples, beribboned with medals,
sit at stone tables staring at chessboards
without pieces and sipping lime liqueur.

When the sun slides beneath clouds thin
as the foam of a receding wave, the blind man

lowers his flute, the girls their baskets,
and the palms begin to sway, one by one,
up from the sea, into that circle
of palms which is like a cage now,
closing so fast not a single bird can escape.

The Creation of the Night Sky

Behind the rising curtains of mist
a small man in a long coat is riding a bicycle
along a cliff: though he can't reach
the pedals, he keeps picking up speed.
Breakers are crashing on the reefs.
A girl wearing goat bells on her ankles turns cartwheels.
In a stone building in bare cells
naked old men are sipping tea through straws.

If there is a city in heaven,
if there is a heaven, one of them thinks,
imagine the marble: brilliantly speckled,
with swirls of silver glittering
against a depthless black.
If there is music—as there must be—
it is played on pianos clear as ice,
tinkling across space, never reaching a human ear.

At high tide the plants swell and the sand
darkens from below, like a bruise.
On the horizon umbrella-shaped clouds are opening.
Then the rain comes: dark lines on a diagonal, lightly smudged.
A bicycle without a rider is negotiating
the winding trail down the mountain.
And in the silence expansive as the seafloor
the stars light up, singly at first, then all at once, blazing.

Part Two

Night Journal

JANUARY 1 – SEPTEMBER 24

The thirty-five calendar entries dividing the poem are the actual dates of its composition. I made these entries, each in its entirety, on the nights listed, in 1996. I only began an entry when I knew I would complete it that same night in one sitting—exactly as I would keep a personal journal. At the same time, the action of the poem occurs on a single timeless night, and the night journal, far from being a conscious compendium of my own worldly activities, is a chronicle of those events which I set in motion in my imagination on the first day of the new year—the traditional starting point for a personal journal. In retrospect, I see that this night journal became far more personal than any such traditional journal I might have kept over those same nine months.

(January 1)

A network of frozen paths.
Then three streets that intersect, like an asterisk,
where hailstones ricochet off the pavement.
From a window draped in blue curtains
a black ball is thrown down,
followed by a terrible cry.
A drunken couple turns the corner,
black and white in evening dress.
The woman is holding a white balloon,
and she teeters while the man
picks up the black ball and flings it
over the rooftop into the next street.
A nurse carrying a bag of lemons picks it up.
For the last hour she has been drinking coffee
and staring up at the three-quarter moon.
She has the image of a hooded falcon
tattooed onto her left wrist,
revealed when she removes her glove
to run her fingertips over the ball,
which feels cool and heavy,
as if it is filled with liquid.
An ice truck passes her at that moment,
driven by a man with a felt cap
pushed back off his shining brow.
Around his neck he is wearing
a chain of gold crosses
and a miniature pocket watch
with glowing red numerals.

His boot feels heavy as cement on the accelerator.
The heater is blowing waves of air
thicker than cotton into his face.
There are no fingers on his left hand.
His head is filled with the broken cries
of birds wheeling over a burning forest
and his heart is beating at the rate
of once every minute.

(January 14)

He has come from a room
in which a blind woman in a black hat
served him boiled potatoes laced with palm oil
and calabash soup in a cracked bowl.
He sat alone at a square table
eating with a wooden spoon
before lighting a thin cigar
with a wooden match from a box
picturing the King of Sweden on horseback
in a blizzard four centuries ago.

(January 15)

The blizzard approaching the city now
is burying the foothills of Pennsylvania
and the mountains of Virginia,
black waves of flinty snow disappearing
into the black waves of the Great Lakes

that are tipped white, capped with ice,
a blizzard that left a hundred people dead
in Chicago and ten thousand stranded
without heat or power in Indiana.
From the radio there is a blizzard
of words which the driver turns off.

(January 27)

The terror of death while under the anesthesiologist's cloud;
or in a free fall with all the sound
in the world switched off;
or violently dizzy when the blood
in the head rushes into the body's extremities
the instant before the guillotine falls;
or in a room without doors
at the center of a house with no address
where gas is seeping from a stove
that cannot be turned off:
every man, in seconds, can become
fluent in the language of fear.
But the man who steps from the curb
at the intersection of two dead-end streets
as the ice truck turns the corner
feels no fear when the yellow headlamps
swoop up into his eyes, silent explosions,
and the wind blows the hat from his head,
and in a black room under a white blanket
someone who cannot sleep

screams at the moment the truck's brakes squeal.
It is a blizzard, not of snow, but blood,
that sprays the driver's windshield
as the cigar drops from his lips.
And he reaches—instinctively—
for the windshield wiper switch
before screaming himself, the cigar's
ember hissing through his pants,
burning his thigh.

(January 29)

The man sprawled on the pavement is a physician.
Later they will find a tumor the size
of a plum in the back of his head.
And coins from a dozen countries in his pockets.
And a silver toothpick driven into his palate.
Several hours before being struck by the truck,
as he lay in bed in the darkness
beside a woman deep in sleep,
four of his fingers wound into her golden hair,
someone he had never before seen
escaped a prison in his dreams.
A man with a burning key in his palm.
Screaming.
A man with a pocket watch around his neck
and no fingers on his left hand.
The driver of the truck.
Screaming.

At a hospital in which the physician himself
has been operating on people daily,
they wheel him into the operating room
with massive head injuries
at the very hour the blizzard finally arrives,
cold sheets whipping wildly
from the city's outskirts into its interior canyons
as the white sheet is whisked from his body.
The train yards and bridges, statues and parks,
the barred basement windows and the highest
portals of steeples from which caretakers
peer twice a year while tending the machinery
of those same bells that just rang twice, muffled,
across the blanked-out night, the emptying
streets and the alleys that are always
empty where cats are nestled
in the iron recesses of the loading zones—
all of it fast disappearing in the chalk dust,
the lunar powder, the furiously sifted
clouds of mica fine as flour
that are pouring from the lit, leaden sky.
At which time the scalpel slices the physician's skin
and the thin saw hisses into skull bone,
and the masked surgeons, fiercely squinting,
open his brain to the intensely penetrating
lights as the blood sprays outward,
a moist, living rainbow.

Or a red blizzard.
Speckling the nurses' gowns, the doctors' gloves,
the anesthesiologist's pump and gauges.
The blizzard of blood in the physician's head
and the neural impulses propelling the dreams
in his frontal lobe are short-circuited
into a blizzard of sparks become one
with the blizzard of snow
through which the driver
of the ice truck is fleeing on foot now,
far from the scene of the accident
that the police, scouring the neighborhood,
have already classified as a hit-and-run.
And at the end of a street where a line
of pigeons still as marble
huddle beside a chipped marble owl
in the eaves of a gutted fire station,
the driver, head down, his fingerless hand
clutching his felt cap against the sharp gusts,
lurches around the corner and bumps
into a woman holding a black ball
and a bag of lemons, the tattoo of a hooded
falcon invisible beneath her left-hand glove.
It is the nurse, just two blocks
from the hospital where the first filamentary probe
has entered the physician's brain
and where she is scheduled to go on duty
at 3 A.M.,
the graveyard shift.

(February 10)

The driver hurries on, ducking through shadows
blue as ice, down a half dozen uneven steps
into a bar where a single red lamp
burns above a line of brown bottles.
Tattered flags are hung on the peeling walls
and a narrow mirror reflects the eyes
of the solitary patrons: red eyes glowing
from the shaded faces of a man and a woman
wearing blue coats with upturned collars.
The woman's scent catches like smoke
in the driver's throat.
Though the vapor of his breath
hovers before him as it did on the street,
the room is stifling.
He sits down on the only available stool,
between the man and the woman,
where a drink awaits him on a coaster
though there is no one tending the bar—
a red liquid in a hot glass cooled
by green ice cubes which waft
steam fine as pollen when they melt.
Before his fingers close around the drink,
the driver taps a thin cigar between his lips
and the man, staring straight ahead,
passes him a box of matches
on which the King of Sweden
on horseback continues to brave
a blizzard four centuries ago.

But now his long white coat
with its upturned collar, gold buttons,
and black medals has been spattered
with blood, and his mouth is frozen
open, in a scream.

(February 16)

The physician, weightless in a deep blue
sea of ether, returns to his dream
of the stranger with the burning key
in his palm escaping from the prison.
Slowly it comes clear to him.
A prison built at the edge
of an immense tundra under the midnight sun.
Bathed in a cold orange glow,
as if the door of a furnace clear as ice
has been thrown open.
On the near side of the prison
a forest stretches to the horizon.
The fir trees are black, tipped with fire,
threaded by white owls.
Wolves with frozen—crystalline—fur
file through the drifting snow in single file.
And a lone searchlight, big as the moon,
revolves like the hand of a clock,
counterclockwise, stiff, shooting its beam
far across the frozen wastes,
far into the trees,

laying down a pathway
along which no one can escape.
Darkness is the only road to freedom
and it leads nowhere.

(February 17)

In the physician's dream the stranger
is dreaming, too, after he lies down
on a bed of icy pine needles,
gasping for breath after running and stumbling
miles into the forest: a dream
of fish swimming against the current
up black channels with the pinpoint
reflections of stars on the surface,
away from the bottomless bay
where the sunken freighter is still spinning
downward years after hitting an iceberg
blue as lapis speckled with starlight,
like the water,
like the backs of the fish
and their eyes that never stray
to the right or the left
as they slither rapidly past
jagged rocks and the snares of roots.
On that freighter, in an airtight compartment,
the ship's doctor is still sitting upright
at a small table
reading Gray's *Anatomy*

in the yellow glow of a lamp.
Before him a clock with no hands is ticking.
And a silver toothpick rests between his teeth.

(*February 22*)

The prison the stranger has escaped
is laid out in a double helix
on an east-west axis.
The identical cells, with glass walls
and a single red lightbulb,
follow the two spirals in and out,
with correspondences visible only
to the warden in his tower
at the point where the spirals meet:
that is, the prisoners in the two cells
farthest from the center both have red hair
and blue fingernails and irises striated
with filaments of ice, but one limps
with his left leg and the other with his right.
And in Cells #24 and #-24 the women are sleeping
facedown, each with a piece of leather
between her teeth, but in #24 the woman's
left wrist has been freshly stitched
and in #-24 it is the right wrist
that is crossed with an arc of Z's.
Overhead, a three-quarter moon is casting
a sapphire glow, and in the infirmary
two prisoners, a man and a woman,

are being operated on simultaneously,
each of them hemorrhaging from a wound
the surgeons cannot find,
each with a broken nose and long hair—
his black, hers blonde—that coils away
into the darkness beneath their heads;
but in his right hand he is clutching a white pebble
while in her left hand the pebble is gold.
And in the stranger's palm that burning
key emanates every color in the spectrum,
from red to blue—
each for an eternity—
until he wakes up, leaps up,
and sprints through the trees
toward the frozen lake
where the moon is concealed
and no stars shine.

(February 24)

The nurse has come on duty,
scrubbed, gowned, and masked,
and entered the operating room
just as the surgeons are trying to stanch
a hemorrhage deep in the physician's anterior lobe.
At first, the bluish white lamps blind her.
The soft hiss of the machinery,
the broken breathing of the doctors and the other nurses,
the musical clicking of surgical instruments,

the squish and gurgle of blood and tissue:
her ears miss none of it.
The taste of iodine floats at the back of her throat.
And a whiff of pure oxygen in her nostrils.
Her teeth ache in her gums.
Her upper lip beneath the mask is sweating.
As she steps up to the operating table
on silent feet, her eyes locking on the physician's
opened skull, the blood-infused labyrinth
of his brain, the tattoo of the falcon—
visible now on her wrist
beneath the skintight latex glove—
begins to flutter its wings.

(February 27)

The driver is nursing his third drink.
Each one has become hotter than the last
until he can barely sip the red liquid
without biting his tongue.
And when finally he bites too hard
and a drop of blood runs down
his lip into his glass,
the steaming green ice cubes melt
and the red liquid turns clear as water.
It *is* water now, just a degree short of freezing,
cold enough to send a shudder
through his body, like a jolt
of electricity, so that he sits up straight

and hears in the distance, in the icy wastelands
a world away from the close blackness of that bar,
the slow-beating, high-flying wings of a bird of prey.

(*March 1*)

The physician took a series of photographs
at night with infrared film
that will be found in a locked drawer
after his death: a woman clutching a bag
while hurrying across an icy street;
a man with a felt cap changing the tire on a truck;
the same man in convict's stripes zigzagging through trees;
a school of fish veering into shadows, deep underwater.
And a portrait of himself,
snapped with the camera held at arm's length,
in which his eyes are opened wide,
his lips are tight,
and the shadow of a bird's wing
is darkening his brow.

(*March 7*)

The lights in the operating room dim
as the blizzard knocks out the electrical power
in that part of the city
and the hospital switches over to its auxiliary generators.
The surgeons and nurses glance up

at the ceiling for those few seconds
during which a pair of blindingly bright
wings sweep out of the physician's open skull
and disappear through the closed
glazed window, into the snow.
And on the one nurse's wrist
the fluttering of wings becomes more agitated.

(*March 13*)

In the bar where the driver of the ice truck
is blinking hard, trying to fight off
sleep, the bar stools on either side
of his are now empty—
the man and woman in blue coats are gone,
though her smoky scent lingers—
and the single red lamp has gone off.
There is no auxiliary generator in the basement,
just a dusty shelf by a fuse box
on which the bartender, who has appeared
out of nowhere, gropes for a flashlight
without batteries and a candle stub.
After lighting the stub with difficulty,
with a wooden match from the box
on which the King of Sweden sits on horseback,
he holds it high before him,
as in a processional,
and ascends the narrow stairway.
The driver is asleep now,

his forehead pressed into his forearm on the bar,
and his glass filled with smoke
that swirls a column to the low ceiling.
When the bartender drips wax onto the bar
and affixes the burning candle,
the column comes alive—
an amber marble veined crimson,
dark feathery textures frozen within its glow.
Carrara marble is translucent to three quarters
of an inch, but light passes clear through
this marble and emerges in a blur
of wings—of nearly imperceptible
flight—on the other side.
The door opens suddenly.
A curtain of snowflakes, torn on all sides,
flutters into the darkness.
The wind screams.
The door slams without a sound.
And no one has entered the bar.
But the candle has blown out
and the column disappears
and the driver's fingerless left hand twitches
as he lifts his head for a moment,
then lays it down again hard.

(March 16)

He is dreaming.
Along a road where others have placed

colored markers, each color
left by a different person.
Red.
Orange.
And black.
One set of markers will lead him back
to the beginning of that same road;
one to the edge of a frozen lake;
and one to certain death
surrounded by angry strangers.
He is following the black markers,
hoping they lead him to the lake.
Overhead the moon is spinning closer
to the earth, its mountains erupting
into volcanoes, its seas bubbling with lava.
Ice fields flank the road,
prowled by wolves.
Stones in the shape of fruit—
red, orange, and black—
are strewn in the dust.
A voice is calling to him from far away,
riding on the wind
that shuttles past him like a train.
Then he hears a train.
Sees its lights twinkling on the horizon,
emerging from a forest beneath purple clouds.
And he realizes he has gone astray,
and for many miles has been following
the red markers,
his boots wet with blood,

his fists tightly closed,
and the taste of iodine
lining his throat.

(*March 20*)

The nurse holds the small white pan
into which one of the surgeons drops
the tumor the size of a plum
which he has removed from the back
of the physician's brain.
She in turn hands the pan to an orderly
who rushes it to the laboratory for a biopsy.
Where the tumor was growing,
the nurse glimpses a patch
of glowing golden tissue
rimmed with orange blood.
The surgeons agree they have never seen
anything like it, and all of them
around that table staring
into the open skull freeze
as that patch glows brighter and brighter
spinning like a disc of burning glass
blinding them all momentarily
before the lights again flicker and dim
and the blizzard rages on,
enwrapping the white hospital building
in a widening, thickening curtain.

The driver awakens at a corner table
in the bar to the rumble of a train
beneath his feet, below the earth,
in a tunnel winding toward the river.
He doesn't know who has moved him
from the bar stool onto one of two
chairs at the table: before the other chair
which is empty, there is an ashtray
with an unlit cigar, a bottle
of red wine, and a small glass.
The guttered candle has been relit
on a shelf behind the bar,
populating the liquor bottles with rapid
shadows and snaking red ribbons of light
up the mirror in which the driver
can see himself, small and remote,
half his face obscured—vertically—
as if by a finely spun silken web.
Before him, in the mirror, he sees the back
of a man sitting rigidly upright
in the empty chair, a man wearing
a black coat with an upturned collar
and a black hat with a glinting silver
toothpick stuck into its satin band.
Fifteen minutes pass, in which the driver
never takes his eyes off the mirror.
When he does, he sees that the cigar
in the ashtray—its ember glowing—

has been smoked halfway down,
that the wine bottle is empty and the glass full.
When he tries to push away from the table,
the sweat beading on the cold planes
of his face, his boots feel as if
they have been nailed to the floor.

(April 6)

In the operating room, at the end
of those same fifteen minutes,
the nurse shivers as if the wind
buffeting the building with frozen flakes
is passing right through her
and suddenly recalls a moon she once saw,
as a young girl, over a northern lake
during an interminable winter night:
it was gold, with a bright orange aureole,
exactly like the patch in the physician's brain
which the surgeons are now probing
with a precisely calibrated microscopic camera—
invisible to the naked eye—
perched on a splinter of flexible steel
twenty times finer than a human hair.
The camera is transmitting brilliant high-resolution
images onto an enormous monitor
suspended from the ceiling across the room.
At first, the images are of fast-moving cells
alternating with flashes of technicolor snapshots—

a woman's golden hair fanning out
on a white sheet in darkness, and then a rapidly
evolving labyrinth of elastic corridors
and chambers illuminated by electrical sparks—
until the images resolve themselves
into a stainless steel grid, static,
honeycombed with identical cells bathed in red light:
brain cells that are also prison cells,
in a prison laid out in complementary halves,
dual helixes spiraling forever inward,
like the lobes of the brain.

(April 7)

I am in a prison of correspondences
and multiple contradictions,
the physician wrote one night in a journal
that will be found in the locked drawer
with the infrared photographs he took.
I am leaving one labyrinth after overcoming countless difficulties—
blind alleys, dead ends, trapdoors, stairways that double back on
        themselves—
only to enter its mirror-image,
which will be doubly difficult to escape
since my every action must be the opposite
of the complementary action I took in the first labyrinth:
that is, an exit route comprised of a negative chain of events.
This is the only prison in the world
that must be escaped twice.

Except for the human mind, of course, whose byways
must also be negotiated and left behind:
once to attain (or attempt) enlightenment
and again when it quits the body once and for all,
at death . . .

(April 17)

In his next entry, the physician continues
this line of thought, describing
the interior layout of a large sunken freighter
whose cabins, galleys, storerooms, corridors, and cargo holds
form a double helix centered by an airtight compartment
at the point where the two spirals intersect.
While seawater has filled all the other spaces on the ship—
like the cells in a beehive brimming to capacity
except for the queen's chamber at its core—
in this compartment a lamp is still glowing
on a small table, beside a ticking clock
with no hands but a pair of hair-thin shadows
circling its face in opposite directions.
A copy of Gray's Anatomy *lies closed on the table*
with a silver toothpick marking a page near the middle.
From the pages of the book blood has begun to seep slowly
and along its spine thick drops are beading.
The door to the compartment has been locked from the inside,
but the hard straight-back chair before the desk
is empty . . .

The instant she stops shivering,
the nurse feels her pulse flutter beneath the tattoo
of the falcon, hooded still
but nevertheless spreading his wings
while remaining immobile,
seemingly poised for flight,
as the last image transmitted
by the surgical camera flickers onto the monitor:
a small table lit by a brass lamp
on which a book is lying in a neat, circular pool of blood.
The point of view is that of someone
sitting at the table,
whose hand enters the frame slowly—
the steady, well-manicured, powerfully sinewed
hand of a surgeon—and opens the book
to the page marked by a toothpick
(which the hand lifts up and out of the frame,
as if placing it between its owner's teeth),
revealing a glossy two-page illustration
of a human brain within its skull.
Exquisitely detailed.
Utterly symmetrical—a hemisphere on each page.
Red, healthily infused with blood,
but with no sign on either page—
or in any of the four lobes—
of the hemorrhaging that has poured from the book.
What does come clear moments later
is that gold disc, at the rear of the left lobe

(the bottom of the left-hand page),
with its aureole of livid orange
and, at its center, a pair of wings,
silvery-white and diaphanous as snow,
that are just beginning to beat
when the hand reenters the frame,
slams shut the book,
and clicks off the lamp.

(May 3)

At that moment, the candle in the bar flickers out
once and for all, and in the darkness
that envelops him the driver thinks he can see
beyond himself for the first time that night:
can see the ice-slicked streets he sped down
before he came to that intersection
of two dead-end streets, identical in length.
His destination lay at the end of one of those streets,
down a path of impenetrably meshed shadows,
a door for which he held the key, burning
in the palm of his fingerless hand.
The route that nearly led him there,
from one side of town to the other,
he can retrace now, as it appeared
in the conical tunnel his headlamps
drilled through the darkness.
Seen from above, the city he crossed
is divided exactly in half,

symmetrical as a double helix,
and laid out on an east-west axis:
twin grids within spirals that cross
at a black bridge over a steely river.
All the city's residents cross that bridge
at least twice a day, coming and going,
attending to the business of the spirit and the body,
upholding the natural and unnatural order of things,
and with the rarest exceptions,
their destinations on one side of the city
always correspond exactly
to their points of departure on the other.
Leaving #100 24th Street, for example, one will end up at #-100
       -24th Street,
but if a table and chairs abut the left-hand wall
in the room one initially enters at the first address,
they will be placed on the right side
of the last room at the second address.
What the driver saw earlier before crossing
the bridge was mirrored on the other side,
right down to the man stepping off the curb
into the path of his truck.
He also knows that in each sector,
at equal distances from those intersections,
there is a hospital.
But he didn't hit two men that night.
Of that, and little else, including whether or not
his eyes are open or closed
in the close darkness of the bar,
he is sure.

(May 10)

When he first set out, the driver saw
the three-quarter moon hovering
through the bare trees,
crisscrossed by their branches,
hemmed in by narrow buildings
with sagging fire escapes
at the entrance to his own dead-end street.
On successive street corners the same blurred face
stared out at him from the bases of lampposts,
the doors of abandoned garages,
the wooden fences around construction sites:
the menacing face of a man as captured
in violent movement by an X-ray machine;
a face that made the sweat run down the driver's back
as he gripped the steering wheel tightly
with his one good hand
and felt that key begin to heat up
in his fingerless palm;
a face, it struck him, that might be gaping out
the porthole of a sinking ship as it descends to the seafloor;
a face he will soon glimpse (but not remember for hours)
through his windshield in the split second
after the physician steps off the curb:
the face of a man, traumatically rendered,
who is gazing in the window of his own nightmare.

(May 20)

Near the end of his journal, the physician noted
that *the human lung has a capacity for*
three hundred cubic centimeters of air
or two quarts of water.
So all the water drained from the lungs
of a fully drowned man
would equal one gallon.
Whether he drowns in a shallow creek bed
or in one of the deepest canyons
on the seafloor, that one-gallon capacity
will not—cannot—be exceeded.
A man's brain is already ninety percent water,
thus influenced as much as any ocean
by the moon and planets,
with its own ebbs and flows
running the gamut from tranquillity to lunacy.
There is, in fact, so much water already
in a drowned man before he drowns
that afterward he may truly be said
to be one with the water,
to have become water himself,
as some sages advise
when offering a particularly enlightened means
of dealing with the harsh surfaces,
the human and material inconsistencies
of this world
around which it is best
that one flows . . .

(May 28)

As the driver approached that intersection,
slowly inhaling smoke from his thin cigar,
he thought of what awaited him through the door
at the end of the long, densely shadowed path:
a steep flight of wooden steps
with a sharply slanted ceiling
that would graze his head;
an abrupt hallway off a precarious landing
lit by a bare yellow bulb;
a rickety door with a hollow enameled knob
opening onto a low room
in which a woman with bright eyes and loosely flowing hair
would be clearing a glass bowl and a silver spoon
from a round table.
The woman would indicate an ashtray
in which she expected him to extinguish his cigar;
beside the ashtray there would be a matchbox
picturing the King of Sweden unsaddling his horse
in a field under a starry sky four centuries ago.
It is one of those stars that filled the driver's head
in the seconds before he reached the intersection,
growing larger and larger,
six-sided, crystalline, and spinning,
drawing him into its vortex,
blinding him to the road for a few crucial seconds—
an enormous snowflake,
among the first to sail into the city
before the fury of the oncoming blizzard.

(June 15)

The nurse has turned her gaze
on the tray of instruments employed in trying
to save the physician's life:
scalpels, scissors, forceps, calipers, and a bone saw,
all of them smeared or speckled with his blood,
their white-hard steel glinting in the light.
Beside them in a steel basin are cotton swabs,
gauze pads, and crumpled cloths, all blood-soaked,
like the sheet on the operating table, the nurses' aprons,
the surgeons' gowns and their latex gloves—
enough blood, she thinks, to fill not one body but two.
And who is to say that in certain instances,
when events conspire just so,
one man does not carry within him—
as he might carry their fears, hopes, and destructive urges—
the nervous impulses, memories, and even the blood of other people.
Which might explain why the physician,
to the astonishment of the nurses and doctors,
had one blood type listed in his medical records
and another engraved on the identification bracelet on his wrist;
it was the latter type, found in his veins
when he was routinely tested before surgery,
that they had given him in multiple transfusions.
And only later did they discover a medical impossibility:
he had two types of blood,
a different one in each half of his body.
Had they drawn blood from his right arm
rather than his left, they would have found

the type listed in his medical records,
which the nurse happened to share.

(July 5)

That snowflake in the driver's head stopped spinning
at the instant the truck thudded
into the physician's body
and the driver saw everything and nothing—
the fractured glare of lights,
the blackness,
the astonished frozen face falling away to the pavement—
before the spray of blood covered the windshield.
Only now, when he finally rouses himself
from his chair in the pitch-dark bar,
stumbles to the door and plunges into the night,
does the driver also recall the physician's face
as clearly as if he had had the opportunity
to study it for hours through the windshield
that might as well have been a microscope lens
or a two-way mirror or a porthole
on a ship sinking through the sea of dreams.
Now it is this face that fills his head
as he rushes away from the bar,
the necklace of gold crosses
with the miniature pocket watch cold against his chest.
The snow is deep on the sidewalk,
so as he nears the corner he veers into the street,
and racing diagonally across the intersection,

reaches its center nearly breathless
when four pairs of headlights—
each pair speeding down a different street—
descend on him simultaneously.
He freezes,
opening his mouth to scream,
and four sets of brakes screech,
four sirens start wailing,
blue and red lights flash,
but no scream emerges from the driver's throat
as he slumps down,
covering his face with his arms.
The police spill from their cars
and crouch with drawn pistols
and he remains inside the tight rectangle
formed by the convergence of the cars,
walled in by blinding light,
ice beneath his knees
and the snow pouring down
from a sky which seems no higher than the lowest building
whitening his hair—
as it will take thirty years to whiten in prison—
in just a few seconds.

(July 16)

In the appendix to a later (1896) edition of Gray's *Anatomy*,
torn out and pasted into the physician's journal,
it is stated that the brain floats in a luminous fluid—

saline, with strong traces of ammonia—
which during sleep reaches temperatures
far below those of the rest of the body
and at the moment of death
may approach the point
of freezing.

(July 29)

The chief surgeon pulls a sheet over
the physician's head and pronounces him dead.
Attendants are summoned to wheel the body
to the pathology lab.
Surgeons and nurses file out,
faces white and grim when they remove
their masks and skullcaps.
Only the nurse with the falcon tattooed on her wrist lingers,
alone with the body for several minutes
as the operating room lights flicker to a cool blue.
At the same time that she glances at her wrist,
amazed to find the falcon unhooded suddenly
(his golden eyes, impregnated with red sparks,
visible for the first time), the ceiling opens—
like the flat doors in the hold
of a ship leading up to the deck—
onto the blizzard's waves of snow.
A sea of snow, whitecaps and foam,
and deep undercurrents, like marble,
feathered with lines of ice.

A glass stairway drops down from high above
on which an angel of death
in the form of a masked, golden-haired woman
descends extending her translucent hand
and leading the physician's soul from his body;
like a swirl of vapor it rises off the table
and reconstitutes itself, upright, naked, transparent,
with a human outline, up the stairway
without so much as a backward glance.
And they are accompanied by the falcon,
who has taken flight finally,
spiraling up and around the stairway
in ever-increasing circles,
leaving behind on the nurse's wrist
a glowing patch of golden tissue
rimmed by orange blood
that has begun to spin like a disc,
casting a ring of burning light around the room
to deter anyone who might interfere
with the separation of the physician's soul from his body.
But there is no one except the nurse,
standing transfixed as the ceiling closes up slowly
on the ascending stairway and its occupants,
clothed now in robes of snow
beneath the wings of the falcon
who has also gone completely white.
Not until the attendants enter and lift
the body onto a cart and wheel it out
does the nurse move,
unsteady on her feet as she crosses

the hall brushing snowflakes from her gown
and removing it in the empty scrub-down room.
Before the mirror above the deep steel sink,
she unties her mask and peels off
her surgical cap and watches her long
golden hair cascade over her shoulders,
glinting with golden lights.

(August 19)

At a small table in a room off the laboratory,
deep in the hospital's basement,
the pathologist switches on his microscope
and examines a slide containing a drop of the physician's blood.
First, some bits of golden light come clear,
then wispy patches of blue and brown,
as if he is gazing down onto a world
through fast-blowing clouds
which as he adjusts the focus
becomes a satellite's view of an entire city in miniature—
the city in which he himself is sitting at that moment,
where he has lived all his life.
Twin grids within spirals that intersect at a black bridge,
symmetrical as the halves of a double helix,
the city's two parts correspond to the two types
of blood the pathologist has discovered
in the physician's body.
Increasing the power of the microscope,
he goes down and down, below the clouds,

so the lighted windows, streetlamps, and automobile lights—
symmetrically burning on either side of the city—
all at once appear, until hovering finally
above the rooftops, no higher than a bird,
he watches raptly as a lone truck
careens across the bridge at great speed,
its headlight beams vibrating like needles
attempting to penetrate the vaporous darkness.
The truck rounds two corners and proceeds
along a straightaway flanked by spindly metallic trees,
while several blocks away, a tall man in a hat
and overcoat leaves a white apartment building
with a marble cornice and glowing steps
and ambles down the long front walk,
between parallel hedges, to the sidewalk;
by which time the truck has turned sharply
onto a narrow street, around an empty square,
through a traffic circle, and accelerating,
takes the corner into the intersection
of two dead-end streets just as the tall man,
who paused on the sidewalk to turn up his collar
and glance back at a top-story window
in the white building, feels the wind
blow his hat off when he steps from the curb,
into the yellow beams of the truck's lights
and is thrown high in the air,
out of the lights for an eternity
before landing crumpled on the pavement.
Absolutely still.
And the pathologist, switching off his microscope,

pushes his chair back and feels a line
of sweat run a zigzag down his back
and hears a rush of water,
as if the small room is submerged,
the sea exerting enormous pressure
outside its low black walls,
pressing in on his skull until bits of flashing
golden light fleck his closed eyelids
and he tastes a single snowflake, cool and bitter,
that won't dissolve on the end of his tongue.

(August 28)

In the predawn darkness, when the wind
blowing through the city picks up speed
and drops several frigid degrees
as it crosses the river,
the physician's body is loaded into an ambulance
and transported to the morgue
where it will be put on ice.
The ambulance is crusted with ice and snow,
luminous as glass as it speeds
beneath the yellow moons of the streetlights.
The attendant behind the wheel,
an unlit cigar clamped between his teeth,
has the heater turned up full,
blowing waves of air into his face,
so that his eyes smart.
He passes a drunken couple in evening dress

staggering from a bar, the woman holding
a black balloon and the man gingerly
tossing a white ball from hand to hand
within the tight, smoky cloud of his breath.
The ambulance skids through an intersection
of three streets, like an asterisk,
where blue curtains froze in midair
fluttering out an open window,
and then, at the intersection of the two dead-end
streets where the physician's two blood types
still stain the snow and the heel tracks
of his hit-and-run assailant—dragged
from that spot resisting arrest—
parallel the curb, it stalls for a moment.
The engine goes dead,
and in the profound silence before
the attendant, working the accelerator
and ignition just so, brings the engine
back to life and eases the ambulance on its way,
the three-quarter moon disappears
behind the bare distant trees
and a single ray of its light the width of a needle
briefly penetrates a top-story window
in the white apartment building.

(September 3)

In that window, in a trapezoidal room—
the nonparallel walls narrowing

sharply at the head of the bed—
a woman is lying, shivering, in the darkness,
under a white blanket that sparkles like snow.
Beneath the bed she can hear the cold sea
rumble chords from a piano
that has plunged from a great height
into vast depths, and by closing
her eyes the woman can see it,
spinning down and away, ever more slowly,
like a fleck of ice, and then a pinpoint
flaring in the blackness.
Like the pinpoint ray of moonlight
that has just shot through the window
to hit the pillow beside her pillow,
at the exact spot where a man's head,
earlier that night, left a deep indentation.
And in that shadowy hollow
the point of light hovers and expands
into a glowing disc,
like burning glass, and blinds the woman
when she opens her eyes again
and leaps from the bed,
her golden hair spraying out into the darkness,
and lets out a cry so terrible
that the ambulance attendant below
hears it as he turns the corner.
That disc of light on the pillow
where the physician rested his head
in the hours before his death
is in the same spot as the disc

the nurse saw inside his skull
in the operating room when they removed
that tumor the size of a plum.
And now she has seen it again.

(*September 12*)

One property of the double helix
is that it constantly opens and closes,
like the ventricles of the heart,
or the twin lobes of the brain exchanging impulses,
or the DNA molecule linked by hydrogen bonds
that can identify absolutely any human being among billions,
or the two halves of the city
connected by the black bridge with its traffic
of human souls, their goods and machinery,
but not like this prison
which does not open in any way
and from which there is no escape.
The driver of the ice truck, convicted to a life
term for the death of the physician,
is looking through his barred window
across an expanse of drifting snow
past the forest of fir trees, tipped with fire,
to the frozen lake where a falcon
wheels high in the moonlit clouds.
An enormous silence envelops the prison.
A line of wolves circles it slowly,
moving outward, leaving concentric

tracks until they reach the horizon
just as the moon reaches its apex.
In his cell, #100, at the end of a long spiral,
with its three glass walls and single red lightbulb,
the driver has placed the gold crosses
he once wore on a chain around his neck
on the windowsill, centered by
the miniature pocket watch
from which he has removed the hands
but whose numerals continue to glow red.
He has tried to imagine, in vain, who could be
in the cell corresponding to his own—
#-100—at the end of the other spiral.
Every night he fights off sleep,
fights off his one recurring dream,
of fish speckled with starlight
swimming up frigid black channels,
away from a sunken freighter
where, in an airtight compartment,
a man is sitting at a small table...
The driver jumps up in a cold sweat
at that point every time,
throwing off his thin gray blanket,
and never sees the man's face
for more than an instant,
as he once saw it through the windshield of his truck,
the face of a man who will drown
in the icy wastes
in the few seconds left him
between life and death.

And, short of breath,
the cold vapor catching in his throat,
the driver shuffles back
to the window on numb feet
and gazes out as the lone searchlight
from the tower at the prison's center
revolves stiffly, counterclockwise,
bigger than the moon now,
and with each revolution illuminates
the network of frozen paths
that lead up to the forest,
where they disappear.
He will remain there all night,
his head filled with the cries of birds
as a falcon continues to glide
above the lake, inward in diminishing circles
to a single black point pulsing
like the driver's heart once every minute.

(September 24)

In his very last journal entry,
in a razor-thin but steady hand on the night
of his death, the physician wrote:
I have a month to live, at the outside.
I can feel it now, unceasingly, pressing
at the base of the right occipital lobe.
The occipital lobe is pyramid-shaped.
The pressure is wedged into the base

where three planes meet in a single point.
Sending neural streams up into the depths of the cerebrum.
Nothing is more symmetrical than the human brain.
Two hemispheres, each with four lobes,
then the onion tangle of the cerebellum
and the medula oblongata where the spinal nerves cross
so that the right hemisphere governs
the left side of the body
and the left hemisphere the right side.
One impediment, or anarchic growth, in any lobe
and all governance ends.
The occipital lobes control vision.
Already the sharp angles,
the hard edges of things, are softening,
contours are melting in the middle distance,
shadows slide along my peripheries
and dark curtains billow on the horizon
in winds I will never feel.
Overnight, it will all go black,
even before motor control, balance, tactility
in the farthest extremities begin to falter.
Tonight all of them worked in unison,
with only a faint tingle of apprehension—
inseparable from the pleasure I was taking—
as I held her in my arms
under the blue glow of the sheets,
our bodies falling away from one another slowly
and the gold of her hair dimming
like a flame being extinguished before my eyes.
So that now, across the room, beyond the circle

of this lamp's rays, her hair is one with the darkness.
As if she is no longer there.
As if she was never there.
Before closing this book,
locking it in the drawer,
slipping into my coat
and then out into the night
where the smoky scent of the approaching snowfall
hangs palpably as the nets
of honeysuckle and jasmine in summer,
I close my eyes and watch myself descend
one last time along a spiraling stairway,
newly painted a luminous white,
into the bowels of an enormous ship out at sea.
Over my shoulder, the mica of the night sky flashes.
Beneath my feet, beneath the scarred hull,
the dark creatures are gliding up effortlessly
from the icy depths,
and in the cabin that awaits me finally
far below deck, down a maze of corridors,
I lean across the table and switch on
the lamp even while opening my eyes
to switch this lamp off.

It's funny, the places that you find beauty. Used bookstores are where everything lovely resides, I'm convinced. I am seventeen and I have found one of life's most well-kept secrets in the dark & dusty recessess of bookshelv crowded in to tiny attic rooms.